Animals

DODD, MEAD WONDER BOOKS

WONDERS OF
ANIMAL DISGUISES

BY SIGMUND A. LAVINE

Illustrated by Margaret Cosgrove

DODD, MEAD & COMPANY, NEW YORK

For the Weiners—

who share their knowledge and friendship with the author

Contents

1. "Things Are Seldom What They Seem..."

Moths that look like bits of bark, spiders that resemble flowers, crabs that camouflage themselves as sponges, butterflies that masquerade as dead leaves, lizards that pretend to be lichen-covered boughs and fish that imitate seaweed—these are only a few of the wonderful disguises of animals.

Long before the Indians of the western plains wrapped buffalo hides and antelope skins about their bodies while hunting in order to approach game, or soldiers fighting in the jungle learned to wear suits of mottled green and black so that they would blend into the landscape, animals were experts in the art of pretending to be something different. They had to be, in order to survive. Not only is there competition between species for food and shelter but also between each species and its natural enemies. While some animals have special characteristics that enable them to avoid danger—such as the ability of the opossum to "play dead," the keen eyesight of the wild goose and the speed of the gazelle—many species

depend upon their color, shape or ability as mimics to defend them from their foes or allow them to get close to their prey.

The commonest disguise in nature is the blending of an animal's markings with its surroundings. Naturalists call this *protective coloring* and refer to creatures that rely upon coloration to conceal themselves as "cryptic" species. Such camouflage may be merely a *general resemblance*—a similarity between the animal's color and the background against which it is usually seen. Thus, although some tundra tenants wear brown coats in summer and white ones in winter, many Arctic animals are white; most desert dwellers, sand colored; the majority of the residents of grassy regions, green.

One of the most remarkable things about protective colorings is that the same species will vary in color depending upon its environment. Pocket mice found on Arizona larva beds are dark, but those living on the white sands of New Mexico are nearly albino. The white owls of the Arctic have yellowish-buff relations in desert lands, but those in dense forests are brown and gray. Similarly, certain moths, normally brilliantly colored, have become sooty-black in that part of their range covered by soft-coal smoke from industrial plants.

However, some animals, once concealed by their coloration, are now conspicuous because they have changed their habitat. Typical of these are the giraffe and the zebra. Millions of years ago both were forest dwellers, but migrated to the open plain in search of a more abundant food supply. Among trees, the spotted coat of the giraffe blended with the foliage and made the animal difficult to see, while its height permitted browsing on branches. Today, on the African veldt, a giraffe's markings give it no protection beyond breaking up the contours of its body. Moreover, the long neck is of little value when grazing on grass. Similarly, the zebra's stripes, that originally merged with tree trunks, are now less useful and the animal has to rely on its senses of sight and smell, plus its great speed, to avoid danger.

Lines, spots and stripes which make it difficult to distinguish an animal from its surroundings—such markings are called disruptive patterns—conceal many species. The spotted plumage of ground-nesting birds cause them to look like shadows, pebbles or leaves when brooding, while a tiger's stripes make the beast almost invisible when motionless among the stems of plants in the swamps and on the grassy plains it inhabits. Incidentally, the habit of holding still is a most important feature of many animal disguises and is an inherited characteristic among species which depend solely upon markings for protection.

When an animal is an actual reproduction, in both color and form, of a definite object with which it is associated throughout life, its disguise is much more effective. This *special resemblance*

Disruptive or "dazzle" patterns are used during war to break up natural lines

9

makes many insects look like bark, flowers, fungi, leaves, lichen and twigs; gives some fish the appearance of submarine plants or dead leaves; turns tropical snakes into lifelike vines and birds into branches. Besides camouflaging animals, special resemblance often permits predators to lure their prey through their likeness to harmless or desirable objects—many frogs and lizards are trapped by young copperhead snakes, which twist the bright yellow ends of their tails in imitation of the wiggling of worms.

The most complicated disguises in nature are called mimicry—the copying of the shape, color and habits of an offensive or disgusting species by other animals. This masquerading was first observed by Henry Bates, an English explorer of the Amazon jungle. He noticed that certain showy, slow-flying butterflies were never molested by birds, although these butterflies seemed to be the logical prey of birds. Bates correctly concluded that the insects had a bitter taste, but wondered why a few butterflies of a species which the birds did eat were always among those that had a bitter taste. Carefully examining the edible butterflies, Bates found that they resembled their unpalatable companions far more than they did members of their own family. He then realized that the edible

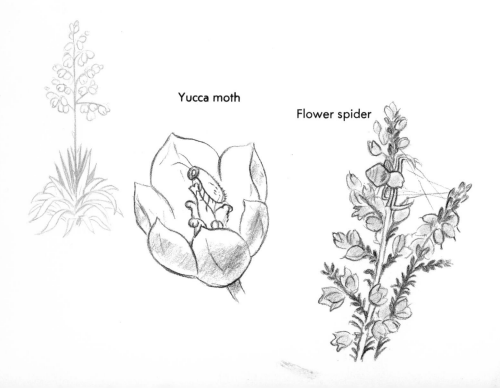

Yucca moth

Flower spider

butterflies had become mimics of the nauseous-tasting species for protection.

While mimicry is rare among mammals and there are few bird, fish and reptile mimics, insects are outstanding imitators. In every case, mimics only copy species that bite, sting or give off bitter secretions. While such animals vary greatly in form, size and structure, their color scheme is universal. Dressed in black and white, orange and black, red, red and black, and yellow and black, they stand out among the browns and greens of nature. Among them are bees, certain bugs, caterpillars and flies, salamanders, skunks, tiger beetles, tree and sea snakes, wasps and weevils.

Just as cautious motorists turn aside when they see a red lantern, other animals shun "aposematic" species—wearers of the above bold colors—recognizing them by their *warning coloration.* For experience soon teaches them that, unlike "cryptic" species, aposematic species are capable of defending themselves or have unsavory flesh. Thus, animals that mimic these undesirable creatures have a much better chance of survival. Such deceptions are particularly easy for the great number of insects whose markings resemble the characteristic black-and-yellow fur coats of many bees and wasps. All they have to do is duplicate the behavior of their models.

Mimics instinctively realize that a mere similarity of color between aposematic species and themselves provides little protection unless they copy the actions of the animal they are pretending to be. Some mimics are outstanding actors. A Brazilian grasshopper that imitates a digger wasp reproduces that insect's habit of running short distances with its wings extended. Even more remarkable are the antics of Indian spiders which mimic black ants. They perfect their impersonation of thrusting forward their front legs, bent at a right angle, and constantly waving them—counterfeiting the conspicuous antennae of ants which are always in motion.

11

Man has long known of animal disguises—the ability of the chameleon to change its color and merge with its surroundings was described by Aristotle in ancient Greece. However, it was not until Charles Darwin suggested that protective coloring and mimicry kept many species from being eliminated by their natural enemies that these subjects were studied scientifically. During their investigations, naturalists have discovered some strange cases of special resemblance: an oriental face on the shell of a Japanese crab; a skull and crossbones on the body of the death's-head moth; and tail markings on the butterfly fish that roughly simulate the Arabic words, *Laillaha Illaha* (There is no God but Allah). More important, experiments and field observations have proved conclusively that many species are able to survive only because of their ability to mimic other species or because of a general or special resemblance to their surroundings.

While it would take many thick books to describe all the disguises animals wear in the great masquerade that is constantly going on in the woods, fields and waters of the world, the following pages deal with some of the most fascinating. First, let's take a closer look at species which are camouflaged by a general resemblance to their habitat.

2. General Resemblance

Pigments, the same substances that make a human's skin black, brown, red, white or yellow, give animals their coloring. If they are in the animal's covering—the hard outer skin (chitin pronounced kí-tin) of insects and spiders, the hornlike hair cells of mammals, or the feathers of birds—the color lasts even after death. Pigments in living cells, however, fade when an animal dies.

While color alone disguises many species, countershading also aids in concealment. This was first pointed out by Abbott Thayer, who noticed that many animals are dark on the back and upper parts, where they receive the most light, while on the lower sides and stomach, where the least light falls, they are much brighter. This makes the animal much harder to see than if it were uniformly colored, flattens its outline and causes it seemingly to vanish under proper conditions.

Although the sharpest sense of animals is sight, the resemblance of many species to their background deceives their foe and prey. For nature's optical illusions are more misleading than those of a magician who makes us think we are seeing a woman sawed in half. Here are some of her outstanding deceptions made possible by protective or concealing coloration. For convenience, each order of animals has been treated separately and is presented alphabetically—a system that will be used throughout this book.

AMPHIBIANS

According to biologists, all animal life originated in the water. Gradually, gills gave way to lungs and prehistoric species crawled onto dry land where, over the centuries, they slowly assumed their

Countershading

present-day forms. However, some animals, although capable of living out of the water, still spend much time in it and always return to their ancestral home to lay their eggs. They are known as amphibians and include: frogs, newts, salamanders and toads.

Because their permanent markings contain movable pigments that can darken or lighten their bodies in response to changes in temperature, touch and moisture, or the amount of light received by the eye, frogs and toads are constantly changing color to conform with their surroundings. In fact, the common frog exhibits more colors than many chameleons. Toads do not have quite as wide a color range, but when one of them squats on a rock it may appear spotted, when it hides in the grass it turns a light green, while in water it becomes a drab olive. However, the most expert quick-change artist among amphibians is a frog native to the Cameroons in Africa. Normally green, it can turn dove gray, gold, maroon, orange, pink, purple and yellow!

The color changes of American tree frogs are not as remarkable

14

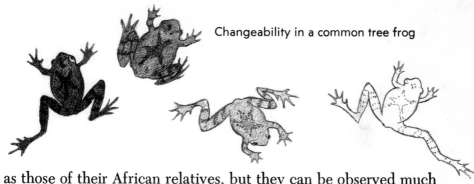

Changeability in a common tree frog

as those of their African relatives, but they can be observed much nearer home. These amphibians (which have adhesive discs on their toes enabling them to cling to bark and twigs) range over most of our country. At times they may be gray, at others brown or green, patterned or solid colored, simulating their environment. It takes a tree frog about an hour to adapt to new surroundings, the ability to do so differing with various species. Nevertheless, all these arboreal acrobats are well camouflaged.

Many toads and frogs don't have to change color to resemble their habitat. Those that live among grasses are generally a bright yellowish green; species that rarely leave the water have olive-green shadings; while others, whose background is dull and dark, are a dirty-brown. Therefore, with their markings and ability to

A little frog of the Congo

Our common toad

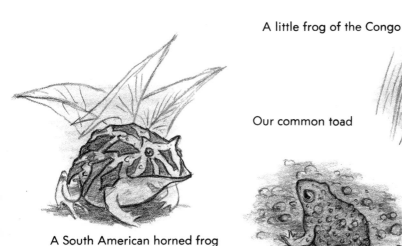

A South American horned frog

change color, frogs—which exist in all parts of the world except the very coldest—are among those animals that are well disguised by a general resemblance to their surroundings. This is especially true in the resting position, for then the markings of many species merge into bands running across the folded leg and foot, so that the frog vanishes into the background.

BIRDS

Because birds migrate from one environment to another, their general resemblance to their environment does not always disguise them. Shadings that protect in one locality may be conspicuous in another. Generally, however, males have bright plumage, females dull—which makes the latter difficult to see when in their nests. Among the exceptions to this rule is the phalarope, a bird that spends most of its life on the open sea. While both sexes are feathered in the same way in winter, the female's summer dress is far more colorful than her mate's. There is good reason. Mr. Phalarope hatches out the eggs and keeps the chicks warm!

While birds show outstanding adaption to their environment— the only totally green birds are found in jungles where leaves never fall—on the whole, resemblance to background is most common among ground-nesting species. Curlew and plover, which nest on pebble-strewn beaches, are speckled; many grass-breeders are striped; the larks and quail of North African and Asiatic deserts are tinted and mottled, making them invisible against the sand, but those that live in rocky regions are dull colored. Although the

Young curlews

South American goatsucker normally has light plumage, those that nest in the boulder-strewn inlets of the Rio Negro are dusty. The only protection the owl parrot of New Zealand has from its enemies is the blending of its dark green feathers, variegated with yellow and brown, with the roots of beech trees growing in mossy glades, for the owl parrot cannot fly.

The disguising coloration of the Antarctic petrel played an important part in the history of military camouflage. During World War I, chemists compounded thousands of gallons of paint for the United States Navy, seeking a bluish-gray shade that would conceal warships on the high seas. Eventually, they were successful in duplicating the color of the petrel's plumage which makes it indistinguishable from the Antarctic Ocean.

While birds (or any other animals) can not think or reason as humans do, they have learned that their color resemblance to their background may not disguise them completely. In order to make their masquerade more effective, some species have developed specialized habits. The eagle owl of the Arabian Desert squats in order to conceal itself, while the screech owl of North America makes itself tall and thin. Unlike Peter Pan, some birds would be delighted to lose their shadows, because they are apt to be spotted by enemies which are otherwise unable to discover their disguises. The nightjar, whose various shades of ashy-grays and browns make it one of the most protectively colored of birds, always crouches low when perching and turns to meet the sun in order to make its shadow as small as possible. Oyster catchers and ringed plover stretch out on the beach with their necks extended, chins and throats pressed close to the sand, for the same reason.

FISH

The fish most effectively disguised by their general resemblance to surroundings are the brilliantly colored species that live among coral reefs where submarine vegetation is brightly hued. How-

17

ever, all fish are outstanding in their adaption to environment.

Most coastal fishes are covered with spines or other appendages that blend with or match the colors of marine plants, rocks, shingle or sand. Beyond the continental shelf—which is merely a submarine extension of dry land—some species, such as flatfish, not only have bodies easily concealed by burrowing in sand or mud but also have the ability to change color rapidly to harmonize with different backgrounds.

These changes are made possible by cells containing black, red, yellow and white pigments that are affected by the amount of light received by the eye and by light-sensitive organs in the skin. If stimulation causes these cells to expand, the pigments flow out from the cells and the fish changes color. When the cells contract, the pigments are concentrated within and the fish becomes paler. Of all flatfish, the flounder makes the most diversified adaptions to the ocean bottom for, in addition to altering its color, this fish can also vary its markings.

Besides flatfish, other residents of the ocean change color to fit their backgrounds. A difference in the amount of light received by their eyes causes many crustaceans, such as shrimp, to undergo a color adaption. The most remarkable color changes in the sea are those made by the cuttlefish and the devilfish—which, despite their common names, are not fish at all, but cephalopods. The cuttlefish

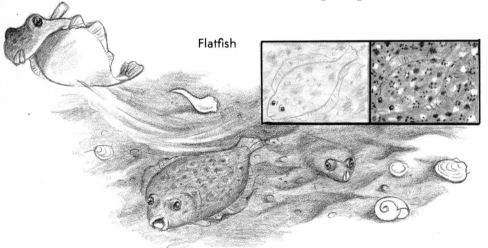

Flatfish

Angelfish

has a huge wardrobe of disguises. Against a white background, it is white; on a sandy bottom, a mottled pattern of light and deep brown; in black surroundings, the mottled pattern deepens; over a dark area containing white objects, the cuttlefish camouflages itself with bold black-and-white squares.

The proper name for the devilfish is octopus. This eight-armed creature has two different disguises. Whenever an enemy approaches, it squirts a cloud of inklike fluid toward its foe from a bag within its body and wiggles to a new hiding place under this "smoke screen." An octopus can also make quick color changes by expanding or contracting its pigment cells, which release shades of blue, brown, green, orange and yellow. These cells may work separately or in combination. As a result, when a devilfish scrambles over the ocean floor, he is able to change quickly from a deep chocolate through dull red and brown to gray. Moreover, as an octopus crawls, its skin humps about obstructions, thus making its body almost invisible. Although the forward motion of the devil-fish is quite slow, the backward movement is much faster than most fish can swim. Its "reverse" speed is due to the ejection, through a tube, of a stream of water from a large cavity within its body—which makes the octopus the original user of jet pro-pulsion.

Many residents of the seashore have a general resemblance to their habitat. None, however, is cleverer in the avoidance of shadow casting than the racing crabs of Portugese East Africa. Extremely well disguised, they would be impossible to detect were it not for the shadow they throw by carrying themselves high off the beach on their long legs—a habit that has earned them the nickname "ghost crabs" because of their appearance in the moon-light. When alarmed, racing crabs hide their shadows by squatting in hollows in the sand.

While fish found in ponds, streams and lakes lack the ability to change color as they swim, many fresh water species are pro-tected by general resemblance. Some, like the speckled trout, have spots that make them difficult to see in pebbly brooks, others have

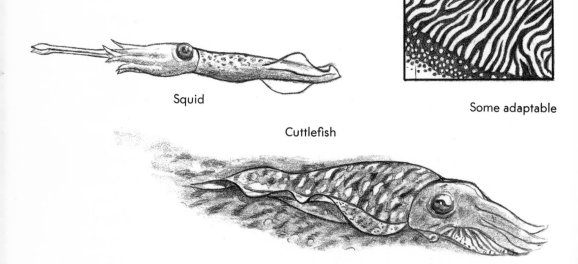

Squid

Some adaptable

Cuttlefish

the same color as the bottom, while still others are patterned to merge with aquatic plants. The hornpout, or bullhead, which rarely rises to the surface, has a black back, while the yellow perch is not only countershaded but has perpendicular stripes that blot out its body when it swims among reeds. If you keep tropical fish, you can easily observe how effective such cross stripes are as a disguise. Watch an angelfish and see how its large, vertical black stripes match the stems of plants. Reverse countershading—a black belly and a white back—conceals an Egyptian fish. This strange color pattern protects a native of the Nile that was once mummified and worshipped in the land of the Pyramids. Because it swims with its belly toward the surface, it is called the upside-down catfish.

INSECTS

No artist's paintbox contains all the colors worn by insects. For these, of all animals, have best adapted to their environment. Thousands of species show a general resemblance to their background, and members of the same group wear different disguises to correspond with their particular surroundings. Thus, tiger

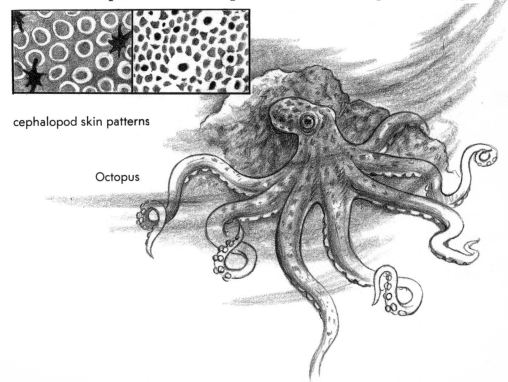

cephalopod skin patterns

Octopus

beetles found along grassy banks are generally green; those living on sandy seashores are pale brownish-yellow; in the jungles of the Far East, velvet-like deep green ones make their homes on wet moss; forest-dwelling species resemble brown leaves in color; salt-marsh varieties are glossy olive-brown, the color of mud.

Grasshoppers show an equally wide range of protective colors that give them a general resemblance to their habitat. The pale bodies of those found in Holland blend with their sandy surroundings; the shadings of those native to Heligoland match the reddish-brown earth of this island off the coast of Germany; the green body and silvery purple back of a Russian species merges into the lush vegetation of the steppes. When these plains become dry and brown, the grasshoppers change their colorful costume for a dull dark one. Another grasshopper that lives in the Middle East can dress in gray, green, red, violet or yellow, depending upon its environment, while changes in light and temperature cause certain strains of the phasmid grasshopper to be brighter during the day and darker at night.

However, color changes are rare among insects. Most species lack chromatophores, the cells that control the movement of pigment. Therefore, insects take considerable time to change color when exposed to a new environment. The process involves molting—the growing of a new skin and the casting off of the old.

Although insects lack the ability to change color rapidly, their permanent coloration affords them excellent protection. Crawling insects are usually black or brown and are thus well concealed when scurrying over the ground, while species that live amidst foliage are apt to be green, due to the chlorophyll in the leaves on which they feed. Insects are not unique in being camouflaged by

22

Chromatophores

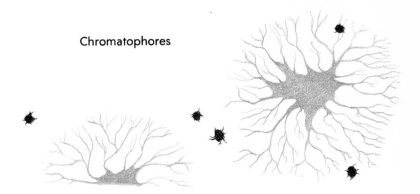

the color of their food. Certain slugs absorb the pigments of the sponges on which they feed, and marine flatworms, fresh water hydras and other transparent animals are also colored by the hue of the food in their intestines.

Because they have eight legs instead of six, and an unsegmented body rather than one divided into three parts, spiders are not insects. They are, however, found in the same environment as insects, for insects are their natural prey. Like their victims, spiders are often protected by general resemblance. Those living on bark are brown; on stone walls, black and white; on sand, tawny; on grass, green. The most fascinating color adaption of spiders is that made by species that live in flowers and become white, pink or yellow, depending upon the shade of the blossom they visit.

MAMMALS

While the spotted hides of the ocelot and jaguar of South America and of the leopard and marbled cat of Asia blend with the sun-dappled foliage of the jungle, all arboreal mammals would be more completely disguised if they had green coats. Unfortunately, no mammal can manufacture green pigment.

Yet the sloth, slowest animal on earth, which lives in the dense tropical forests from Honduras to Bolivia, wears a green disguise. Unable to stand upright on four legs, this helpless creature hangs

upside down from tree limbs, holding on by his strongly hooked claws. When he wants to move, he inches his way along the underside of a bough, traveling about ten feet in an hour—which is why we sometimes refer to a slow-moving person as slothful. Although sloths are incapable of running away from enemies, they do not fear them, for their drab brown coats are covered with green algae and predators confuse them with foliage.

Markings that blend with the background conceal many ground-dwelling mammals. The golden cat, whose bones have been used as medicine by the Chinese for centuries, is almost invisible in the rocky wastes of Southeast Asia because of its reddish-brown coat; wolves vary in color from near black to white, depending upon their habitat—the farther North they live, the lighter they are—while the lion's tawny-buff coat harmonizes with the sandy plains on which it lives.

Often adult mammals are disguised by one color scheme, their babies by another. Naturalists believe that the coats of such young have the same shadings and patterns as did their remote ancestors. When there is a difference between mature and immature mammals, the adults are normally solid colored and their babies usually mottled. The pups of the harp seal are an exception to this general rule, but there is a satisfactory explanation. The wooly white pelts of these youngsters make them inconspicuous on the snow-covered ice packs of the North Atlantic, where they are unprotected while their mothers go fishing. When the pups are old enough to recog-

nize danger and flee, pale gray hair replaces their original pelage.

No baby animal is better disguised than the fawn of the Virginia deer. A fawn's ability to remain motionless for hours, when hidden under a bush by its mother, and its white-flecked "vest" fuse it into the surroundings. In fact, Virginia deer, from birth until death, are among the best disguised of all animals that rely on general resemblance for protection.

Although these deer have poor eyesight—they confuse any downwind object that is stationary with the rest of the landscape— they do have keen senses of hearing and scent, great speed and power to leap fifteen or twenty feet in a single bound. Moreover, as adults they wear brownish-gray coats in winter, which, with their countershaded bodies, make them difficult to distinguish among bare bushes and saplings. While their summer dress of reddish-brown does not provide as effective a disguise, it still helps conceal them in heavy foliage.

Because some mammals change color, they always have a resemblance to their background. Hares, rabbits and weasels, among others, bear dark fur in summer and white fur in winter. Strangely, only one rodent changes pelage seasonally. This is the collared lemming, which also has another distinction, that of being the only mammal which sheds its claws once a year. While seasonal color changes by mammals usually mean turning white in winter, there are exceptions. The pine squirrel, one of the few really wild creatures of European woods and the only representative of its

family on that continent, has a long winter coat of grayish-brown fur, which is shed in May for a short red one.

Scientists have learned that, while a rise or fall in temperature causes some mammals to change color, the decrease in the amount of light received as the days grow shorter brings about an inability in many species to produce pigment, and thus the hair turns white. This explains why there are so many white animals in Arctic regions where sunlight is never strong. The importance of light in seasonal color changes has been proven by many experiments. In one, Russian scientists took thirty polar hares which had assumed winter coats and exposed ten to varying amounts of artificial light, keeping another ten in darkness and ten more in intense artificial light. In March, the first group was summer-coated, in June the second lot was still white, while the third ten turned brown in January.

REPTILES

Homochromy, the color resemblance between an animal and its habitat, is very common among reptiles, particularly snakes. If you have ever seen a smooth green snake in a field, you appreciate why this harmless creature is called the "green grass snake." A related species, the rough green snake, is just as well disguised, for its light green back and pale yellowish body made the "vine snake" hard to see in shrubbery. Thus, the same coloration conceals both arboreal and ground species.

Usually ground snakes are covered with spots, stripes, dots and

26

other markings that cause them to vanish when still in colorful surroundings, but which attract attention when the snakes glide over a dull surface. Snakes also have warning coloration. Just as red means stop, and yellow, caution, on a traffic light, the red and yellow rings encircling the body of the southern coral snake signify danger. This species is one of the most venomous snakes native to the United States.

Through trick photography, a television performer can go behind a screen dressed in one costume and reappear immediately wearing another. Far more remarkable is the ability of many lizards to alter color instantaneously to match their surroundings. These changes are made possible by pigment cells in the skins which respond to variations in temperature, humidity or the amount of light received. Of all lizards, the chameleon of the Old World has the greatest skill as a quick-change artist, although others, including tropical geckos and Asiatic agamids, make rapid color adjustments. Incidentally, the "chameleons" sold at circuses and fairs are not chameleons at all but anoles, natives of the southern United States—and, while they can change color, their power to do so is not equal to that of the true chameleon.

Desert lizards are often striped to match the weathered rock

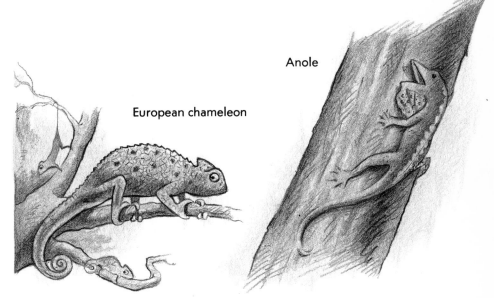

Anole

European chameleon

and sand on their range, but the misnamed horned toads—they are actually lizards—are extremely well disguised. These animals are remarkably equipped for desert living—their nostrils close up tight when they burrow in sand, just as a seal's do when it swims under water. Some species lay eggs; others give birth to living young, but all have fascinating habits. Perhaps the most unusual is the ability of certain species to squirt blood from their eyes for several feet. While all of them bear a general resemblance to their environment, the round-tailed horned lizard is the best camouflaged.

Round-tailed horned lizards may be yellowish-gray, ashy white or various shades of light brown, depending upon their surroundings, for they have the ability to change color. Their disguises are coupled with a set pattern of behavior when frightened. First, they flatten out on the ground and remain motionless, then suddenly dash away, stop short and seemingly vanish into the sands of the desert.

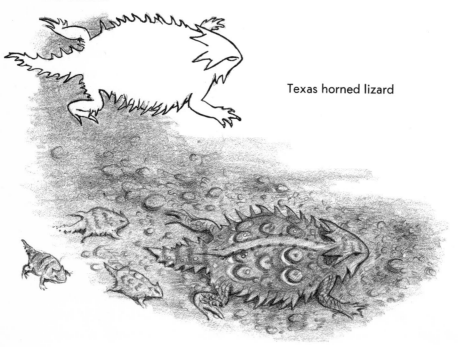

Texas horned lizard

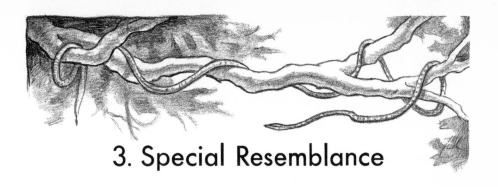

3. Special Resemblance

Although background-matching coloration disguises many animals, the species that actually resemble a particular object found in their habitat have far more protection. An insect that looks like a leaf has a much greater chance for survival than one whose green body merely blends with vegetation. Similarly, while disruptive patterns aid many snakes to merge into their backgrounds, certain tropical snakes are far more successfully disguised. Their brown, gray and green bodies, narrow, pointed heads and long, tapering tails give them the appearance of living tendrils or dead vines entangled in trees. Thus, *Oxybelis* is not only concealed by color and shape but by a special resemblance that makes it easy for this Honduran snake to deceive the chameleon upon which it feeds. Unlike other arboreal species, *Oxybelis* does not hang from a tree but extends the fore part of the body horizontally and holds it motionless in space unless the wind blows. Then the snake sways back and forth like a bough whipped in a breeze.

As in the case of general resemblance, insects lead in the number of species that are disguised by special resemblance. Nevertheless, other animals are protected by some of the most unusual examples of this type of camouflage.

AMPHIBIANS

If you should happen to hear the sound of hammering coming from one of the sphagnum bogs that dot the coastal plain from New Jersey to Georgia, don't wonder what is being built in such a location. For the "hammering" is the call of the carpenter frog, one of the most difficult of all amphibians to see when swimming, because its color matches exactly the brown-stained acid waters of the bog.

Not quite so hard to spot, although well disguised, is the pine woods frog whose markings resemble the bark of the yellow pine, a common tree throughout this amphibian's range. Certain tree frogs also have a special resemblance to bark, their bodies being mottled with a disruptive pattern that looks like lichen. However, the outstanding case of special resemblance among amphibians is that of a South African frog. Its upper body is speckled with dark blotches as are many dead leaves, while its underside is a chestnut brown which gives the impression that it is a leaf shadow. The frog adds to the semblance of a leaf by keeping its body depressed.

BIRDS

Commonly called the "pump handler" because its outlandish call sounds like the noise made by an old-fashioned wooden pump handle, the bittern has excellent protective coloring. Its body is the

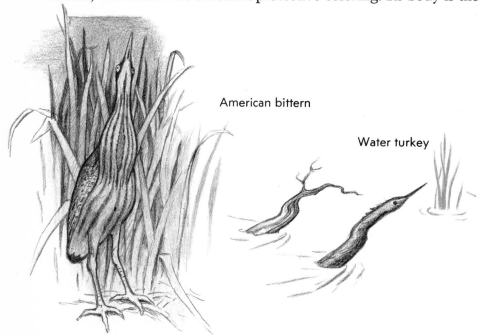

American bittern

Water turkey

Tawny frogmouth

same shade as the rushes and reeds among which it lives. Moreover, this bird can also disguise itself as a cattail. When an enemy approaches, the bittern stands with its body stiff and upright, with head pointed upward. To avoid the danger of being discovered in rustling weeds, the clever bittern swings from side to side in the same direction as the breeze, first with its neck and head, then with its whole body—resembling true nodding cattails.

You wouldn't want to eat a water turkey for Thanksgiving dinner, because these inhabitants of the bayous along the Gulf Coast feed entirely upon fish, which gives their flesh an unpleasant taste. However, their natural enemies consider these strange-looking birds with slender, snakelike necks and long tails a most delicious meal. As a result, water turkeys must constantly be on guard against attack as they sit in dead trees with their wings half spread, drying out their feathers, which, unlike those of ducks and geese, do not repel water and soon become soaked. Because they have excellent eyesight, water turkeys can see an approaching predator some distance away. When alarmed, they drop like stones into the water, then stick their long necks stiffly above the surface, holding them absolutely motionless, so that, even to the most keen-sighted marauder, they resemble sticks jutting out of the mud.

Not only does the plumage of the American nightjar, the frogmouth of Sumatra, and the Indian tree swift resemble bark, but the rigid roosting posture of all these birds gives them the appearance of a broken branch. While the nightjar (whose disguise is particularly effective as its open beak and eyelids look exactly like

31

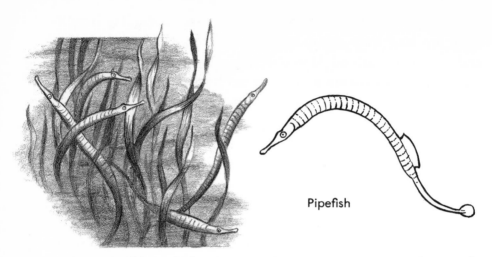

Pipefish

cracks in bark) and the frogmouth never doff their bark-bough camouflage, it is only worn by swifts when they are fledglings. As adults, these strong flyers rely on their wings rather than any disguise for protection.

FISH

Special resemblance disguises many fish. Some, like the scorpion fish of the Indian Ocean, look like rocks. Others, such as the triggerfish and pipefish, simulate swaying vegetation. The former's tapering body, mottled green coloring and habit of standing on its head in eelgrass, holding fast with its sucker-like mouth, disguise it perfectly. Instead of resting upside down, pipefish grab hold of underwater grasses with their prehensile tails to achieve a leaf effect. They also resemble marine plants when in motion, for they swim vertically with their heads upward.

Still other fish have the appearance of seaweed. Among the best camouflaged is the Australian sea dragon, a relative of the sea horse, which lives among the seaweed on the coral banks or Indo-Pacific waters. A very poor swimmer—like the pipefish it travels in an upright position through the water—only ten inches long and with no means of defense, the sea dragon cannot escape its enemies. However, it has a wonderful disguise. Extending from its body are long leafy appendages that reproduce the shape, color and texture of seaweed. Moreover, the sea dragon has a prehensile tail that it hooks around a plant, an act that not only completes its camouflage but keeps it from being swept away by a current.

The frogfishes found in the Sargasso Sea, those "submerged and bottomless meadows" in the western Atlantic between the Azores and the southern coast of Bermuda, are excellent examples of special resemblance. In the sargassum, which is so thick that legend claims that ships caught in this seaweed never get clear, frogfishes swim safely because their color and form blend so completely with their surroundings. Fleshy protuberances and weedlike filaments extend from their bodies, the disruptive patterns of which look like the fronds and berries of the golden sargassum.

Special resemblance to vegetation is not confined to salt water fish. The leaf fish of the lower Amazon Valley is not only colored and shaped like a leaf but acts like one—not even moving when netted. The *peche de folha,* as the Brazilians call it, hangs head downward beneath the surface or lies flat in the dead foliage on the river bottom with its transparent fins tightly flattened against

Australian sea dragon

33

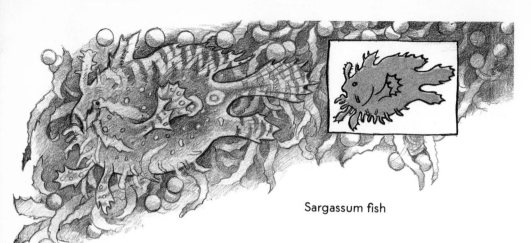

Sargassum fish

the body. But when a smaller fish approaches, the "dead leaf" suddenly opens its large mouth and swallows the passer-by in one gulp.

Besides fish, other residents of the world's waters have special resemblances. Certain crabs are masters of disguise and, unlike other animal masqueraders, wear masks. Using their pincers as scissors, these crabs cut algae and sponges into pieces, chew on them for a few minutes—probably to cover them with a sticky secretion—and then place them firmly on the hornlike bristles that cover their upper shells. Each species of masking crab has its own techniques—some merely cover their heads, others their entire bodies, still others their first pair of legs—but no matter what their system, when they have finished disguising themselves, all look like marine plants.

Whether in coastal algae or seaweed, Aesop prawns always resemble their environment. Green when in eelgrass, red amidst ruddy vegetation, violet in coraline algae, or speckly brown or orange to harmonize with other growths, they can also give themselves a special resemblance to *Melobesia,* an algae whose shadings range from pink to violet. When the prawns settle on a leaf spotted with *Melobesia,* they imitate the spots exactly and even form the opaque stripes that are characteristic of this growth.

34

Leaf fish

INSECTS

Resemblance to Leaves

A special resemblance to their food plant or resting place camouflages many insects. This is particularly true of species that wear a leaf disguise—a very common one in nature's masquerade. While various insects reproduce definite long, broad or withered leaves, some merely display their wings and assume the general appearance of a leaf. The similarity is startling, for leaves are normally flat, having either an oval or a toothed edge—which corresponds to the shape of many insects' wings.

If you examine a leaf you will find that it is crisscrossed by veins branching off from a midrib. By shifting the veins on the edge of their wings, some grasshoppers simulate the veins on a leaf; certain butterflies fold their wings in such a manner that their colors give the illusion of vein; while moths vary in the methods they use to counterfeit them. Some species, including the geometrid moths of South America, have a false midrib across their front wings and when resting on a stem cover their conspicuous hind wings with the camouflaged front pair—although moths usually settle with all four wings extended flat. Both moths and butterflies that pretend to be leaves attempt to make their bodies thinner by tilting them. They also alight in a position that will throw the smallest possible

35

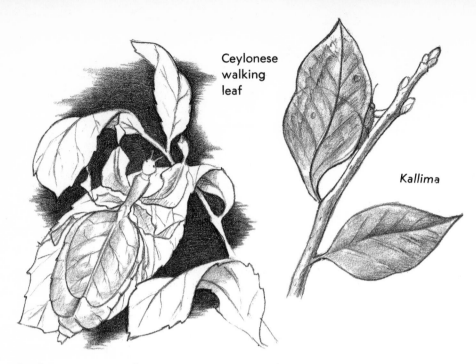

Ceylonese walking leaf

Kallima

shadow. Species that cannot make themselves appear thin frequently try to pass as crumpled or torn leaves.

A butterfly always rests with its fore wings raised. This is to conceal the hind pair, because, while the upper surfaces of all four wings are brightly colored, they are usually drab on the underside. The broad bands of metallic blue and yellow that make the *Kallima* of India one of the most beautiful butterflies in flight magically vanish when it lands and folds its wings above its back. In this position, *Kallima* appears to be only decaying vegetation, because of the white spots on the underside of its wings that resemble fungi. This is the source of this insect's common name—"the dead-leaf butterfly."

The wings of many other butterflies are patterned in like manner. They not only resemble fungi but also discolored, diseased or half-eaten leaves. Typical is a Brazilian butterfly that is partly green in color, with brown vein markings in its wings which approximate the torn end of a leaf.

Like butterflies, grasshoppers also have specialized leaf resem-

A dead-leaf caterpillar   Leaflike grasshopper and butterfly

blances on their wings, although many merely simulate fresh or dry vegetation. One species has a unique disguise—it looks like a burnt blade of grass. Another, native to South Africa, escapes hungry birds and reptiles through its likeness to a tobacco leaf.

As you know, caterpillars are not worms but the larvae of butterflies and moths. The word "caterpillar" is derived from *chatepelose,* an Old French word, which means "hairy cat." While some caterpillars are covered with thick fur coats, others have bodies covered with humps, horns and spines. This makes it possible for many green caterpillars to camouflage themselves as leaves. The humps on the back of the prominent caterpillar closely resemble the ragged edge of the leaves on which it feeds, while the long, thin pine measuring worms which live among evergreens appear to be part of that tree's needle-like foliage.

Many other species besides butterflies, grasshoppers and moths have a leaflike disguise. Some of these so-called leaf insects constantly move when suspended from a plant stalk to make their impersonations more convincing. They rotate their bodies on two or three legs, suggesting leaves about to fall. However, of all leaf insects, the disguise of the Ceylonese walking leaf is the best.

Cousin to the praying mantis, one of the most ferocious of insects, the walking leaf is a gentle, defenseless eater of vegetation. Despite this, no insect is in less danger from its enemies, for the walking leaf is camouflaged from egg to maturity. The egg looks like dried-up, spiny seeds. When the young emerge, they are wing-

37

Walking stick

less and a glossy red that matches marvelously the buds at the end of the branches where they feed. A full-grown walking leaf's green body is shaped and veined exactly like a leaf, as are the green wings that lie flat over it. Moreover, the legs are flattened and look like leaflets that have been nibbled by caterpillars, because they are covered with yellow stains and have ragged edges. The walking leaf's disguise is so perfect that East Indian natives believe these creatures are really leaves that have been turned into insects by magic. Although secure in their disguise, these masqueraders take no chances—so, just as the bittern sways when the wind rustles the weeds in a swamp, a walking leaf wiggles back and forth when a breeze sets the leaves dancing.

Of the 250,000 species of beetles described by naturalists, none are more destructive than the smallest members of this tremendous group, the weevils. These are pests on cultivated plants and do great damage to stored cereals. Usually dull-colored, some of them resemble bark. One tiny species rolls off its tree-trunk home when alarmed, draws in both legs and antennae which fit into receptacles, and looks just like a pebble or a pellet of earth on the ground. Another weevil, the Malagasy of Madagascar, has a remarkable resemblance to lichen and, when a swarm of these insects bunch together on a bough, they look more like plants than animals. Madagascar is also the home of another lichen masquerader, the Malagasy bug. Not only do its flattened wing covers have a distinct lichen pattern, but they also have shadow-reducing flaps.

Resemblance to Twigs

Did you ever see a twig with legs? If you have sharp eyes you can find one almost anywhere in trees and bushes, for the *Phasmatidae* family is a large one. Commonly known as walking sticks, these insects are disguised all through their lives. Most walking sticks live in trees, and when the female lays her eggs—they look like small flat seeds—she drops them to the ground singly where they remain all winter and hatch out the following spring. The eggs hatch in a remarkable fashion. Their tops lift up like the hinged cover of a coffeepot! The babies are grayish-green in color, but at maturity become gray and brown. Thus, they are always protectively colored: green when leaves are green, brown when they are brown. Moreover, when the foliage drops, the long, thin walking sticks with their slender legs are easily mistaken for a cluster of dry twigs.

Walking sticks show great adaption to environment. Those that live in tall grasses simulate grass stems and change color as the blades fade. Others have a remarkable similarity to the prickly stems of the thorny bushes on which they live. One species, native to Borneo, is covered with leafy appendages that make it appear to be a moss-covered twig.

Which "twig" is the caterpillar?

A twiglike
moth

At dusk you may be startled as a stubby twig suddenly begins to wiggle along a plant stem or tree branch. Don't be alarmed—the "twig" is really a caterpillar. Disguised both by shape and color—green stick caterpillars remain on green twigs, brown ones on brown twigs—these insects hold their bodies out at an angle from a perch and duplicate a twig in form, position and shading. Stick caterpillars remain motionless all day long, but shortly after sunset begin to feed on vegetation. Because they have only two pairs of legs on their abdomen, these insects crawl with a strange motion that has earned them the nicknames "loopers" and "measuring worms." Some young people believe in the superstition that they are going to get a new outfit if one of these caterpillars alights on them. They also think that, as the insect crawls over their bodies, it is taking measurements.

Resemblance to Flowers

By co-operating, some insects are able to disguise themselves as flowers. What appears to be small pink petals fluttering to earth in the forests of South America is really a flight of butterflies with glasslike front wings and pink-spotted hind ones. On the other side of the world, an African species settles on stems in great numbers and turns them into flowering plants.

However, no disguise through massing is as effective as that of bugs belonging to the genus *Flata* found in British East Africa. Either green or red in color, when these insects settle on a plant they arrange themselves so that the green ones look like unopened foxglove buds, the red ones like blossoms!

Certain crab spiders also resemble flowers. A South American species, that has a most unspiderly shape and a body covered with white knobs tinged with pink, looks like a flower petal. Another, found in North America, not only simulates flowers in form but perfects its disguise by changing color to match the bloom of the plant on which it rests. In fact, spiders' disguises are among the

Ant bear

most deceptive in nature. Some of them actually cover their bodies with moss or dead ants to camouflage themselves!

MAMMALS

An ant bear looks nothing like the animals Goldilocks visited, for these natives of the low, swampy savannahs along South American rivers are different from any other living creature. They have long pointed snouts, tall, thin forelegs, humped shoulders, huge bushy tails and tremendous tongues which they use as brooms to sweep up the termites on which they feed. Though slow moving and easily cornered, ant bears can defend themselves with their strong, curved front claws, but are helpless when sleeping. Therefore, when an ant bear decides to take a nap, he curls his four-foot body into a tight ball, wraps his grayish-brown tail around it and sleeps securely, disguised as a pile of dry grass.

Both young and adult Malayan tapirs are protected by special resemblance. The babies of this wild relative of the domestic pig have dark brown coats dappled with overlapping snow-white bars and dots that make the youngsters indiscernible and cause them to have the appearance of sunlight seeping through the shadowy thickets in which they hide. Black on the forequarters, head and hind legs, with the rest of their bodies from the shoulders backward a dirty-white, adult tapirs at rest on the jungle floor closely

41

resemble gray rocks with the sun shining on them.

While the brown and gray coats of most monkeys make them invisible when crouching in a tree, one of the most boldly colored, the guereza, whose home is in the dense forests of equatorial Africa, is also well disguised. Its jet black body, white bushy tail and the mantle of foot-long white silky fur that surrounds its face so resemble hanging white lichen that the guereza is rarely seen by other animals, as this monkey rarely descends to the ground. Although animals are deceived by its camouflage, man penetrated it easily. Before the end of the last century, hunters had killed over two million guerezas to supply trimmings for ladies' hats and coats. Fortunately, monkey fur became unfashionable before the species was exterminated, and now guereza pelts are used only by witch doctors in their ceremonies.

REPTILES

Geckos are common lizards in both the tropics and subtropics of the Old and New Worlds. The reason for their widespread range is that they frequently stow away in cargoes at one tropical seaport and are carried to another—most of the species in this country being immigrants. Like flies, geckos can walk up a smooth wall or across a ceiling due to pads on their toes, while their claws permit them to climb trees.

Some geckos change color to harmonize with their environment; others are marked like the bark of the particular tree to which they cling motionless during the day. Still others have the appearance of lichen-covered bark. Both the fringed gecko and the lichen-bark gecko have a scalloped fringe that covers the sides of their bodies and legs. When pressed closely to the bark, this fringe wipes out their outlines and prevents the casting of shadows.

The disruptive patterns of many lizards imitate foliage and jungle mold as well as bark and lichen, but the most remarkable special resemblance among reptiles is that of certain tropical snakes. Their deformed heads look exactly like twigs!

fringed gecko

4. Alluring or Aggressive Resemblance

Not all animals disguise themselves for protection. Some use camouflage to lure their prey. The pink tongues of certain turtles, when wiggled, fool many fish into thinking they are worms, while masking crabs leave their bright pink-and-white pincers exposed and seize any small fish that mistakes them for food.

The master of alluring disguises is the praying mantis, who well might be called the "preying" mantis. Although this insect keeps its forelegs raised as if in prayer, it is really poised to seize a victim. Always hungry, mantids—it is equally correct to say mantises, mates, or mantids, the last being favored by naturalists—are fiercely predatory creatures, which will, in order to satisfy their appetite, eat their mates.

Getting enough food is relatively easy for female mantids of a Burmese species. Part of her neck resembles a flower petal and its underside is shaded a light lavender with pink edges. Throwing back her head, the female faces the sun so that the light will fall on her and awaits the approach of nectar-loving insects. Her deception is enhanced by her trick of swaying her abdomen from side to side as if the wind were tossing a blossom. Moreover, her extremely flattened legs appear to be dead foliage. Other mantids in Africa and Asia also resemble flowers or bark or twigs.

Many insects wear grotesque disguises to scare their enemies. Their resemblance to something frightening is often made more realistic by false eyes—technically known as eyespots—that simulate actual ones. Eyespots also divert the attention of marauders from the real eyes and are frequently located in the wing tips or

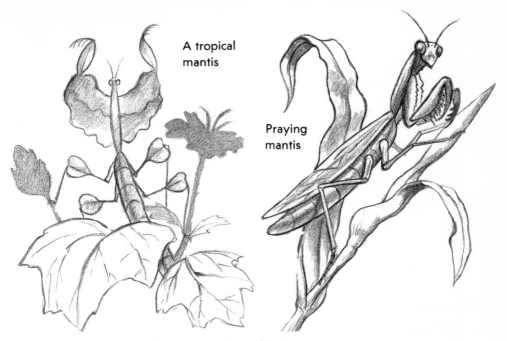

A tropical
mantis

Praying
mantis

other body parts that can withstand damage. Strangely, eyespots
are common to such vastly different animals as birds and insects.
Thus, both the peacock and the peacock butterfly sport false eyes
and display them when courting their mates.

Because many lizards have the power to cast off and replace
injured tails, great numbers of them use their appendages to turn
an attacker's attention from vital parts of their bodies. Some species
have brightly hued tails—although the rest of them is dark—and,
when these are pounced on by a predator, the lizards break them
off and make their escape. In time, they grow new tails. One lizard,
a close relative to the gecko, has a unique use for its tail, arranging
it so that it resembles a head instead! Certain butterflies also counterfeit a false head at the wrong end of their bodies. An eyespot
and a projection that looks like an antenna on each hind wing make
their "heads" extremely lifelike.

Several caterpillars have outstanding ability to make themselves

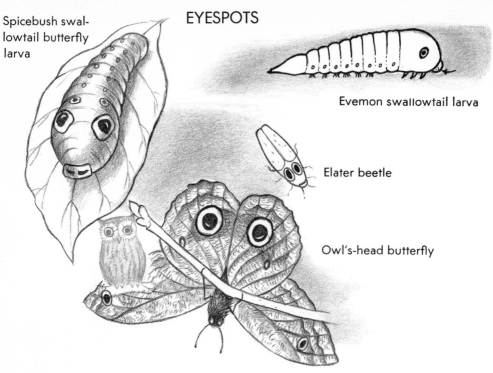

Spicebush swal-
lowtail butterfly
larva

Evemon swallowtail larva

Elater beetle

Owl's-head butterfly

look terrifying. Those of hawk moths not only resemble twigs when motionless but become "snakes" when alarmed. Holding on to a stem with their hind legs, they rear their bodies to display a dark band that simulates a snake's back. As they do so, two eyespots appear, portions of the body become inflated and the head swings back and forth in snakelike fashion. Many other caterpillars resemble repulsive reptiles when disturbed, as does the alligator bug of tropical America. A large hollow projection in the front of this creature's head makes it look like an alligator's snout, complete with teeth, when seen from the side, while a dark line gives the impression of slightly opened jaws. Many of the sphinx caterpillars, whose name is derived from their habit of rearing back and raising their front legs so that they have a likeness to the famous Egyptian statue, assume threatening positions. With a swollen forebody, a horn on its tail and glaring eyespots, one of these harmless caterpillars looks most menacing.

The Atlas moth of the East Indies, one of the most beautiful and largest members of its family, has a remarkable semblance to a cobra when its wings are folded. The markings, shape and position in which the wings are held reproduces vividly the head, eye, mouth and "spectacles" of the jungle's most deadly reptile. Another strange special resemblance is that of a butterfly found in Central America. When this insect alights upon a dead branch, its folded wings, with their eyespots and mottled brown and gray under-surfaces, transform it into an owl—hence its name: the owl's-head butterfly.

Some animals try to frighten their enemies by increasing their size. They gulp in large amounts of air and inflate their bodies. As indicated, various caterpillars do this, as do chameleons, several fish, a South American frog and a Siamese toad, when disturbed. An even stranger disguise is that of "playing dead"—for along with the opossum, this habit is found among yellow-bellied toads and hognose snakes. While the toads turn over to show their warning coloration—they have bitter flesh—the snakes are merely bluffers. These harmless reptiles put on a wonderful act when approached.

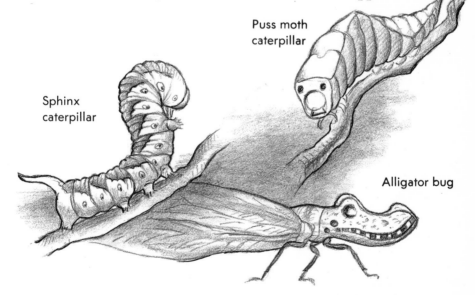

Puss moth
caterpillar

Sphinx
caterpillar

Alligator bug

They flatten their heads and necks, hiss loudly and inflate their bodies with air. If this performance fails to drive the intruder away, they roll over on their backs, open their mouths, shake a few times, then lie as if dead. It is a most convincing exhibition, but if you turn a hognose snake right side up, it will immediately roll over and "die" again!

Inflated puffer fish
and toad

Opossum and
hognose snake
"playing possum"

5. Mimicry

Skill in mimicking a dangerous or inedible species enables many animals to survive. Although many harmless water snakes closely resemble venomous ones in coloration and ape their behavior, the crested rat imitates the porcupine, and the friar bird pretends to be the oriole, insects are the best mimics. Here are only a few of their wondrous impersonations.

STINGLESS BLUFFERS

Strangely, just as only female bees, hornets and wasps can inflict painful stings, only the females of other species mimic them. These impersonators are remarkable, for they move, run and fly in the same way as does the insect they are imitating.

This means that the actions of mimics are totally different from the normal behavior of their group. While most moths are night flyers, those that model themselves on day-flying butterflies are active when the sun shines. There is also a physical difference between a mimic and its family. Moths that copy wasps have transparent wings; those that do not, have scales on theirs. Species of Asilid flies that masquerade as carpenter bees have broad, hairy

bodies with pigmented wings, while those that are not mimics have slender bodies and transparent wings.

Often defenseless insects merely have the general appearance of stinging ones: Sometimes they resemble a particular species. In any case, mimicry goes beyond form and color. Thus, when touched, many moth and beetle imitators of bees and wasps bend their abdomens around and jab them against their annoyers. Still others carry their imitation farther—they have a slender extension from the rear of their abdomens that simulates the long ovipositor of certain wasps.

Syrphid flies have two common names. They are called flower flies because they are fond of nectar and pollen and frequent flowers. They are also known as hover flies, as they seem to suspend themselves in mid-air over a blossom, their wings vibrating so fast that no motion can be detected. These colorful insects are of great importance in the cross-pollination of plants, being second only to the bees in this regard. Oddly enough, a great many species of Syrphids are skillful mimics of bees. Other members of their family imitate wasps. Their impersonations are so clever that even

Moths that mimic
hornet, bumblebee and wasp

entomologists—students of insect life—have difficulty in telling a Syrphid from its model. Those that pretend to be bees have stout, hairy bodies and play their parts so well that they even reproduce the characteristic buzzing of the honey makers. The wasp masqueraders have the same seemingly bare bodies as their models and show great skill in copying flight patterns. Incidentally, certain Syrphids live with social bees as tolerated guests. In return for free rent, they act as scavengers.

No Syrphid is more interesting than the drone fly. Its larva was named the rat-tailed maggot in the middle of the Eighteenth Century by Reaumur, although a much better name would be the snorkel maggot. The larva's tail lengthens and shortens like an expanding spyglass so that its tip will extend above the surface and allow the immature insect to breathe while feeding under water or in a carcass. Drone fly larvae often mature in decaying animal matter and look very much like bees when they emerge as black-and-yellow adults. Hence, for hundreds of years, men thought that bees swarmed spontaneously from the bodies of dead animals. Many ancient writers, including Virgil and Ovid, recorded this

Two flies that mimic bees

A fly wasp-mimic

True wasp

myth as a fact and it was firmly believed in most nations until well into the Middle Ages.

While it isn't easy for a grasshopper to mimic wasps—although some do—it is an even more difficult feat for a fly. There are two reasons. Flies have only two wings—wasps and bees have four. Moreover, both bees and wasps have much longer antennae than flies. However, because of their coloration and acting ability, many flies do have a striking resemblance to those stinging insects. Some have even evolved long slender bodies and clublike abdomens to reproduce the "wasp waists" of their models. Others, handicapped in their impersonation by short antennae, try to carry them as high as possible. But the calobta fly of South America is not concerned with the length of its "feelers"—it has white forefeet and waves them constantly when in a resting position, in perfect mimicry of those of a wasp.

BEETLE BUGABOOS

Though tiger beetles have long, sharp jaws and are thoroughly capable of defending themselves—and prove it by flaunting aposematic colors—many of them mimic similarly marked bees and wasps. Yet, other insects mimic tiger beetles. Among them is a defenseless Borneo locust that imitates not one but three different tiger beetles! When very young it looks and acts like a tiny species; in mid-growth it resembles a slightly larger one; at maturity, still another of considerable size. This mimicry is so exact that several of these locusts were placed in a museum display case and labeled "beetles." Some time later, an expert going over the collection accurately identified the creatures as locusts.

While many long horned beetles have coloration that gives them special resemblance to bark, lichen, twigs and withered moss, those that visit flowers are clever wasp mimics. Other longhorns imitate ants and, in some cases, their performance is so successful that they are able to live unmolested with their models.

True bumblebee

Cuckoo bumblebee

An optical illusion enables a Borneo beetle to pass as one of the wasps that are parasites in the larva of vegetation-destroying moths. Wearing the typical red-and-black warning costume of a Braconid wasp, this beetle has a white mark on the side of its abdomen that gives the impression of a wasp waist *in profile*. This is a remarkable hoax, for the thin waists of Braconids are hidden by the position of their wings when viewed from above.

While there are many mimics of bees and wasps, the strangest of all is a bee that imitates other bees. Known as the cuckoo bumblebee, this insect is a parasite, like the bird for whom it is named. Just as the cuckoo lays her eggs in the nests of other birds, this bee enters the underground nests of the hard-working common bumblebee and sets up housekeeping. Excellent mimics, the intruders usually have no difficulty, but occasionally these masqueraders are unmasked and either killed or driven out by the rightful owners of the nest.

ALMOST "ANTS"

Despite the fact that ants are extremely narrow waisted and wingless except during the mating season, they are often mimicked by insects that are most un-antlike. Among species that impersonate ants are: various bugs, beetles, flies, grasshoppers, moths and spiders. The most marvelous ant mimicry is done by spiders. If it is not easy for a two-winged fly to imitate a four-winged wasp, it is doubly difficult for a spider to pass itself off as an ant, as its body is not segmented. Yet, by constricting their abdomens and duplicating the characteristic motions of ants, many spiders convince their natural enemies that they are ants and capable of biting.

Velvet ants—which are not ants at all but wasps with a very potent sting—are wondrously imitated by spiders in Ceylon. Their mimicry is so perfect that male velvet ants are often confused and think the disguised spiders are true females and try to court them!

Although grasshoppers are stoutly built, they are outstanding mimics of ants. One of the reasons for their successful imitations is that they are extremely clever in adapting their antennae to resemble those of their models. As a matter of fact, grasshoppers can also make their antennae appear as part of the background. One species has the ability to make its antennae look like blades of grass, another like sticks, still another like stones.

A number of grasshoppers—and some beetles—give the illusion of having thin waists like ants because of their color pattern. One grasshopper, found in the Sudan, has the narrow waist and swollen abdomen of an ant superimposed in black pigment upon its body. The rest of the body is light in color and therefore quite difficult to see in the glaring sun. Another African grasshopper which lives among ants when young appears to be narrow waisted because of three pairs of bright spots that draw the eye away from the rest of its body. Sometimes, two diagonal stripes give the impression of a waist, as in the case of many beetle mimics of ants.

Nothing in the tropics is more engrossing to watch than the parade of leaf-cutter ants, in which every marcher carries a "parasol" over its head. These sunshades are triangular pieces of leaves

A spider that mimics an ant

54

which they carry to their underground nests for use as topsoil in their fungi gardens. Although these ants are heartily disliked by planters because they can strip a stand of citrus trees of their foliage in a few hours, a bug common in the jungles of Guiana pays them the compliment of mimicking them. The bug faithfully reproduces its model, including the leaf-umbrella held over the head. The leaf is represented by the bug's flattened body which ends in a sharp, jagged edge suggesting a roughly gnawed leaf. Below the "leaf," the brown feet and head of the bug appear to be those of an ant.

The strangest of all ant mimics is the larva of a beetle that preys upon these insects. After eating his model, this masquerader avoids detection by species that prey on it by placing the head of its victim on its own shoulders like a mask!

BUTTERFLY AND MOTH MIMICS

Lepidoptera, the second largest order of insects, consists of about 100,000 species. Found in every part of the world except Antarctica, butterflies and moths are among the most beautiful of insects. Often harmful in the caterpillar stage, as adults they are either harmless or beneficial to man. A large number of butterflies and moths, particularly those native to the tropics of both the Old and New Worlds, are master mimics.

While butterflies only pretend to be other butterflies that have some form of protection, moths impersonate other insects. Day-flying moths that visit flowers frequently imitate net-winged beetles whose acrid body juices make them most unpalatable to other animals. Oddly, several North American insects that have the same warning coloration as these beetles and equally inedible flesh also mimic them. Because they resemble one another in appearance and engage in the same activities, these insects gain collective protection and their chances of survival are greatly increased.

Hummingbird moth and hummingbird

Wasp moths, as their name implies, resemble wasps in appearance. While it is pure coincidence, their two sets of wings are joined by the same type of tiny hooks that connect those of bees and wasps, making it possible for them to work together in flight—a physical characteristic totally different from that of other moths. Moreover, they wear the same dress, and the hind legs of wasp moths have yellow scales that accurately reproduce the pollen baskets of worker bees. Many also have a false ovipositor. While some members of this family look like a specific wasp, others merely have a general resemblance to their models. However, all faithfully duplicate the actions of wasps, particularly when in the air. The hornet clearwing, common in eastern North America, looks exactly like one of the quick-tempered hornets that dress in black and yellow, while the peach borer, which does so much damage to fruit trees in its larval stage, is difficult to distinguish from certain steel blue and orange spider wasps. An even harder task is to identify some of the Castniids, tropical dwellers in both hemispheres, for even nonmimetic species look more like butterflies than moths.

You may have seen, hovering over nectar-laden flowers in midsummer, what appeared to be an extremely tiny humming bird. However, if you were quick enough to net this green-and-brown gem, you'd have found that it wasn't a bird, but a moth. As you examined the hummingbird moth, you'd find it difficult to believe that it was an insect and not a bird—that instead of feathers, it had six furry legs.

Monarch butterfly

Viceroy butterfly

The most complicated cases of mimicry are found among the butterflies of the New World. Here, Heliconiids and Ithomiids—which are among the most highly protected of insects because of their rubbery bodies that can withstand a great deal of abuse, their bitter-tasting flesh, unpleasant odors and warning coloration—fly fearlessly from flower to flower. They are mimicked by dozens of moths and other butterflies, so that a collector cannot tell whether he is seeing a model or a mimic until he nets a specimen. This mimic-model relationship is made even more complex by the fact that many of the imitators of Heliconiids and Ithomiids have one or several protective characteristics.

You probably have seen monarch butterflies, for they are great travelers. While quite a few butterflies make a one-way migration, the monarch is the only one that makes a round trip. In the fall, tremendous numbers of them mass together and fly south, stopping at night, as did their ancestors before them, in certain trees in huge swarms. After spending the winter in a semiactive state, they fly northward in the spring in groups of twos and threes. On the way, the females lay their eggs on milkweed plants—each new generation continuing the northward flight. Because they have a very bitter taste, due to their milkweed diet, monarchs are rarely attacked by insect-eating birds. Experiments have proven that after

Coral snake

a bird has bitten into one of these insects it never touches another. Therefore, the butterfly that mimics the monarch—the aptly named viceroy—enjoys the same protection.

Thus, by mimicking other species, many defenseless animals are able to escape the claws, jaws and beaks of their natural enemies. It would be extremely difficult to choose the winner of the grand prize in nature's masquerade because of the skill and cleverness mimics display in order to survive. However, a serious contender for the honor is the caterpillar of a West African moth. It is preyed upon by parasites which lay their eggs in its body after boring through the cocoon in which the caterpillar changes into a moth. When the eggs hatch, the tiny parasites devour the caterpillar and spin a cluster of small, frothlike cocoons for themselves on the outside of the original one. To protect themselves against this unhappy fate, the caterpillars produce a mass of frothy, cream-colored bubbles which they wrap in strands of silk around themselves while spinning their silken tents. As a result, the cocoon looks as though it had already been invaded!

6. Discovering Disguises

In order to see animal masqueraders you don't have to go to tropical jungles, the steppes of Russia or descend into the clear waters of a coral reef. For if you have keen eyes and great patience, you can unmask many of them in your own back yard, in a city park, an open lot or along the sea shore. Nothing is more fascinating than to watch a "twig" turn into a caterpillar; a "thorn" assume its rightful shape as a tree hopper; or to note how coloring and mimicry protect many species. Make sure you observe accurately and make notes of what you see, for there is every chance that you may uncover an unrecorded disguise. However, even if this never happens, you'll have a wonderful time discovering the marvelous ways animals camouflage themselves in order to survive.

Index

Sigmund A. Lavine

was highly active while in college; he wrote features for the Boston *Sunday Post* and covered Boston University sports for two wire services. His parents were permanent members of John Craig's famous stock company, so, quite naturally, he played leads in Shakespeare productions and stage-managed five annual presentations of the Gilbert and Sullivan Association.

After receiving his M.A., he taught in a United States Government Indian School at Belcourt, North Dakota, for two years, learned to speak both the Sioux and Cree languages and talk in sign language. He was invited to tribal dances, ceremonies and Indian Court in reservations throughout Canada and the Northwest.

Sigmund Lavine has taught in the Boston Schools for over twenty years and is now an assistant principal. He also lectures and writes literary criticism.

With his wife, their teen-aged son Jerrold, Carrie, their whippet, and Andrea ben Ghazi, their prize-winning Afghan hound, he lives in a house filled with books, fish tanks and historical china. His family enjoys cruises to South America, cross-country motor trips and truck gardening on a piece of rocky New Hampshire land.

Minneapolis Public Library

The borrower is responsible for all books drawn on his card and for fines on his overdue books. Marking and mutilation of books are prohibited, and are punishable by law.